Sprout朋友们

By Rebecca Wilson Schwengber

Illustrated by Katrin Haerterich

Copyright © 2017 Language Sprout Publishing, L.L.C.
ISBN: 978-1-63354-004-0
All rights reserved. Published in the United States by Language Sprout.

languagesprout.com

One to One Giving

Language Sprout envisions a world in which every child is equipped with multilingualism.

For each Language Sprout Book you purchase, we will give one to a child in need.

Research has shown how important access to books is in a child's development.
For many around the world, books are inaccessible.
With your help, we are partnering with schools around the globe to provide colorful books to kids in need.
Thank you. Together we can change the world.

To find out more and to
Join the Language Revolution[TM], please check out our website.

www.LanguageSprout.com

To Gabby, Zelda, Eli, Bobby and Charlotte. You are the inspiration for everything!

Welcome to the Sprout Friend Series

Hello! Welcome to the Language Sprout Community. My name is Rebecca Wilson Schwengber and I am the founder of Language Sprout.

As a mother of five and a foreign language educator, I understand the importance of having good support for children throughout the learning process. That is why I created the Sprout Friends series.

The Sprout Friends series is part of the Language Sprout curriculum. Each book uses familiar characters to build lesson upon lesson so that beginning language learners feel connected and successful to the text that they are reading. In additon to our books, we proudly offer workbooks, flash cards and many games to accompany each lesson.

We really hope you enjoy this series. Please email any comments or questions to hello@languagesprout.com. and check out www.LanguageSprout.com for information on more products and classes to aide you in your language learning journey.

Ciao,

Rebecca Wilson Schwengber

AZAM!

你叫什么名字?

Sprout朋友们

Pepé

Emma

Marta

和

SH

叫。。。

Bob　　　Lulú　　　Lily

AZAM　你叫什么名字?

Visit us soon in our next book...

跟Sprout朋友们一起数数

www.ingramcontent.com/pod-product-compliance
Lightning Source LLC
Chambersburg PA
CBHW080444090526
44586CB00047B/2497